T0198413

A Word Is A Seed

WestBow Press books may be ordered through booksellers or by contacting:

WestBow Press
A Division of Thomas Nelson & Zondervan
1663 Liberty Drive
Bloomington, IN 47403
www.westbowpress.com
844-714-3454

ISBN: 978-1-6642-7821-9 (sc)
ISBN: 978-1-6642-7820-2 (e)

Library of Congress Control Number: 2022917082

Print information available on the last page.

WestBow Press rev. date: 09/20/2022

WESTBOW
PRESS®
A DIVISION OF THOMAS NELSON
& ZONDERVAN

A Word Is A Seed

By Erica Jo Cartrett

A word is a seed
That you plant in the air
It floats out of your mouth
And can fly anywhere

A word comes from someplace
That's hidden inside you
A place where you choose
And believe what's to guide you

A word can be funny
A word can be smart
A word can forgive
And create a new start

A word can be quiet
A word can be loud
A word can be humble
A word can be proud

A word can be sweet
A word can be gentle
A word can be angry
Or mean or resentful

A word can be hopeful

A word can be wise

A word can be truthful

A word can tell lies

A word can encourage
And make people smile
A word can be witty
And delivered in style

A word can be medicine
Good for the heart
A word can upset
And break friendships apart

A word can be sung
A word can be yelled
A word can be whispered
Right into a shell

A word can be bitter
A word can be sour
A word can be lovely,
Like a sweet-smelling flower

A word can be rude
And make people cry
A word can be difficult
To say when you're shy

A word can inspire
And spark a new trend
A word can be brave
When it's time to defend

A word can bind up
A word can set free
A word can throw mountains
Right into the sea

A word can create
Something genius and new
A word can inform
And reveal what is true

The more words you say
The more seeds you plant
So say words that help
Anytime there's a chance

Say words that will comfort
And words that are good
Say words that will make
People feel understood

Say words that are kind
And honest and pure
Say words that don't put down
But lift up and cure

Say words that make peace
Not ones that cause pain
Say words that refresh
Like a cool summer's rain

A word holds the power
Of Life and of death
So each word's important
With every breath

Sometimes a word's timely
Sometimes a word's not
So pause and think twice before
You say a lot

A word is a seed
That you plant in the air
It floats out of your mouth
And can fly anywhere

A word is a seed
You plant as you go
Each one builds belief
That blossoms and grows

Belief comes from hearing
And blooms in your soul
Where your heart meets your brain
And you form what you know

And whatever you know
Shapes how you see your days
So create something beautiful
With each word you say

Printed in the United States
by Baker & Taylor Publisher Services